Cameracolour Cameo

Cambridge

Photographs by *JOHN BETHELL*

Text by *PHILIP SCOONES*

A member of the Ian Allan Group

First published 1984

ISBN 0 86364 006 0

Published by Town & County Books, Shepperton, Surrey;
and printed by Ian Allan Printing
at their works at Coombelands, Runnymede, England

Graphic reproduction by NG Graphics, Bromley, Kent.

INTRODUCTION

Gowns grave, or gaudy, doctors,
students, streets,
Courts, cloisters, flocks of churches,
gateways, towers.
              Wordsworth, *The Prelude.*

The visitor who takes a punt from Magdalen Bridge on a summer day and floats gently along the Cam past what Henry James described as 'The loveliest confusion of gothic windows and ancient trees (which looks as if it had been turned on for ornamental purposes)' may be little inclined to ask himself too many searching questions about Cambridge's origin. However, once he has returned his punt, that first bridge, the Great Bridge, will begin to provide the answer just as it provided Cambridge with its name.

Four Roman roads met here and the river itself is navigable from King's Lynn via the Ouse up to this point. The Romans built west of the river under Castle Hill, and Bede mentions an Anglo-Saxon settlement, which he calls Grantchester. The bridge was across the river Granta and the town appears in the Domesday book as Grentabridge. It is supposed that the Gr became C because the Normans found the former difficult to pronounce. Thus the town and the river changed their names. The river above the King's Mill is still called the Granta and flows down from the Granchester where Rupert Brooke lodged and for which he longed in the horror of the trenches.

William I on his way south from York in 1068 stopped at Cambridge and ordered the building of a castle. The castle has gone, but the Castle Hill has remained the administrative centre of the county. By the 13th century the market town south of the bridge had become more important and from Milne Street, parts of which survive in Queen's Lane and Trinity Lane, lanes or hythes ran down to the river where the goods brought from King's Lynn were unloaded. This bust-ling trade reached its climax every year at the end of August and the beginning of September when one of the greatest fairs in Europe was held just outside the town at Stourbridge.

The modern traveller approaching the city from Newmarket might well notice the Pye electronics factory and Cambridge airport and miss the tiny Norman Chapel belonging to the Leper Hospital of St Mary Magdalen. In 1211 King John granted the hospital the right to hold an annual fair. It was at about the same date that he granted this right to the Augustinian priory of Barnwell to hold Midsummer Fair, which continues to this day on Midsummer Common between the Newmarket Road and the river. When Daniel Defoe visited Stourbridge Fair in the course of his *Tour Through The Island of Great Britain* in 1724 he was deeply impressed by the size of the deals that were made. Wool and hops he called the 'peculiars of the Fair' and he noted that 'there is scarce any price fix'd for Hops in England till they know how they sell at Stourbridge Fair'. John Bunyan, had earlier taken it as the model for Vanity Fair in *Pilgrim's Progress*.

Two years before the granting of the Royal Charter to Stourbridge Fair a band of scholars fleeing from the riots between 'town and 'gown' in Oxford came to Cambridge. Whether Cambridge had already begun to develop a university by this stage is a matter of conjecture and dispute. It has been suggested that the great monasteries of the Fens such as Croyland sent monks to lecture at Cambridge, but this idea is now generally treated with some scepticism. However tender a plant it may have been at the time of the influx from Oxford the university soon grew and acquired status. The troubles of the University of Paris contributed a fresh supply of students in 1229, and in 1231 we see the King issuing writs relating to the University. In 1333 Pope Gregory IX gave the Bishop of Ely authority to absolve scholars who had

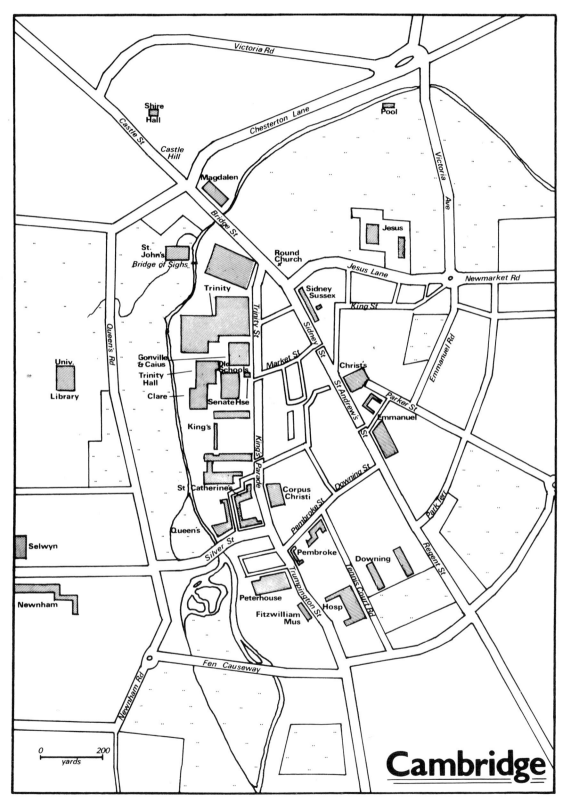

Cambridge

shown physical violence to one another.

Many of these early pieces of evidence refer to matters of discipline or of property and thus we can observe the pattern being laid lown that was to be repeated for many centuries. There was tension between university and ecclesiastical authorities, there was rivalry within the University between students from the north and south, and persistently throughout the centuries there was antagonism between 'town' and 'gown'.

A medieval university was known as *Studium Generale*, the body of teachers gathered together and licensed to teach. It was as such that Cambridge was recognised, at King Edward II's request, by Pope John XXII, and with that recognition its doctors gained *Jus ubique docendi* the right to lecture throughout Christendom. Both Oxford and Cambridge had schools of theology perhaps as a result of the presence of the friars. In 1256 William de Kilkenny, Bishop of Ely, left 200 marks to Barnwell Priory for the provision of two students of theology in the University of Cambridge 'to say Mass for his soul'.

His successor at Ely, Hugh de Balsham, took a step of great significance, when in 1284 he followed the example of Walter Merton at Oxford and founded the first college, Peterhouse, to comprise a master and 14 fellows. However, during the first two centuries it was the University which was far more important than the colleges. In 1226 we find references to the Chancellor of the University who was to be elected by the Masters, regent and non regent. Thus, from the very beginning Cambridge established itself as a university where authority lay in the hands of the teachers, not the students. From among the regents two proctors were chosen with wide-ranging powers to control both the discipline and the finances of the University. The proctors still exercise some of these functions and many undergraduate activities come under their control and supervision.

An undergraduate normally came to Cam-

The Market Place in 1842.

5

bridge at the age of 14 or 15 and was expected to be able to read and write, have a little Latin and some *grammatica*. He embarked upon the trivium of grammar, logic and rhetoric, of which logic was the most important. He attended disputations in the 'Schools' and learnt to 'respond' to questions. After five years he could 'determine' by being examined and then standing in the 'Schools' throughout Lent waiting to answer anybody who wanted to dispute with him. He was now a bachelor of arts and after following the quadrivium of arithmetic, geometry and astronomy he could proceed to a mastership. At 'Commencement' the aspiring master had to defend himself against the youngest regent, non regent and doctor of divinity. His subject could well have been, *Whether angels can read the thoughts of men*.

These scholars did not, for the most part, live in the colleges at this early stage. Hostels were the normal dwellings and these were strictly controlled by the University. Many of these hostels were later to be subsumed into the new college foundations. In the hostels the students paid their own way, while the colleges benefited from the endowments of their founders. The popular image of the indigent scholar is not accurate. Most came from the middle and several from the upper ranks of society. In the story of Godshouse, later to become Christ's College, in the 15th century we see two developments which pointed the way to the future. The college began to accept 'pensioners' who would pay a rent for their chambers, and also to organise lectures. From these beginnings grew the tutorial system and the large undergraduate body of which the scholars of the original foundation came to represent only a small part.

The 15 years between 1337 and 1352 witnessed a great spate of college foundations. In 1337 Edward III founded King's Hall, the young scholars of which were known as the King's Childer, and began a long tradition of royal foundations and endowments. Clare followed in 1338, Pembroke and Gonville Hall both in 1347 and Trinity Hall in 1350. In 1352 a licence was granted for the foundation of Corpus Christi which uniquely among Cambridge Colleges was founded by a town guild, the Guild of Corpus Christi. This desire to put the benefits of commerce to the futherance of scholarship found a generous echo in the recent history of Cambridge, when the Cambridge businessman John Robinson devoted the fortune he had made from the rental of television sets to the foundation of Robinson College. The violence between 'town' and 'gown' which had so frequently disfigured the history of Cambridge looms less large when one contemplates these instances of noble co-operation.

The account books of King's Hall give us a picture of its life. It had a vineyard for the pruning of which it had to pay a man a penny, but it seems likely that only vinegar was produced. The garden was carefully tended, and there are frequent entries referring to the brewery and the stables. Colleges also baked their own bread and laundered their own clothes. This self-sufficiency cannot have endeared the colleges to the town.

The next foundation which came only after the passage of a century in 1441 dealt with the interests of the town in the most high handed manner. The heart of medieval Cambridge was swept away for the sake of Henry VI's grand plan at King's College. It has left us now with Cambridge's greatest monument, but to the tradesman and householders of the 15th century the effect must have been as devastating as the comprehensive redevelopment schemes of today.

A scholar at King's College was not allowed to go beyond the college gates unless he was accompanied by a Fellow, another scholar or a servant. He could exercise himself within the college precincts. The college had bowling greens and tennis courts, perhaps even archery grounds. The college codes which demanded this exclusive way of life also sternly forbade any vanities in clothes or behaviour. The fads and fancies which made the medieval academic wince would probably elicit a similar reaction in a modern tutor. Red and green shoes were out, and long hair and beards were frowned upon. Dogs, falcons and hawks were not to be kept. Bears are not specifically proscribed, presumably because the compilers of the codes had not considered the possibility of a choice of pet as outlandish as that which Byron made four centuries later.

The great royal foundation at King's was

Town v Gown in 1820.

quickly followed by another at Queens' in 1446. Catherine Hall, later to be St Catherine's College came in 1473, founded by a provost of King's College, Robert Wolark. In 1496 Jesus was the first of the colleges to take over a monastic foundation, in its case a nunnery. In the first years of the new century the great John Fisher was responsible for the carrying to completion of two more foundations with royal connections Christ's College in 1505 and St John's College in 1511, both the gift of Lady Margaret Beaufort, mother of Henry VII. Fisher in a sermon preached before Henry VII spoke of a 'weariness of learning and study' but he was the chief among those who brought about a regeneration of the intellectual life by the introduction of the 'New Learning'. He brought the great Dutch humanist Erasmus to Cambridge. Erasmus wrote in 1516, 'It has flourished to such a degree that it can now compete with the chief universities of the age.'

This academic revival took place alongside the great religious upheaval which involved Cambridge very directly. Thomas Cranmer, a fellow of Jesus and Hugh Latimer, a Fellow of Clare, developed their Lutheran ideas along with William Tyndale at the White Hart Inn, nicknamed 'Germany'. Soon however, debate gave way to persecution which destroyed proponents of both sides of the argument. Fisher himself was executed in 1535 because of the line he took on the royal divorce and his successor as Chancellor of the University, Thomas Cromwell met the same fate five years later. Cranmer and Latimer both died for their faith as did Nicholas Ridley, once Master of Pembroke, who at the moment of death lovingly recalled the orchard at Pembroke where he had learned all the epistles by heart, and then proclaimed, 'Farewell therefore, Cambridge my loving mother and tender nurse!' Today his memory is kept alive at the college in the name of a path, Ridley's Walk, by the Master's Lodge.

Despite the sad violence of the times new foundations continued to appear. The old Monk's Hostel was refounded as Magdalen College in 1542 and Henry VIII himself founded what was to grow into the largest college at either Oxford or Cambridge, Trinity College. Two friaries provided sites for completely new foundations in the reign of Elizabeth. In 1584 Sir Walter Mildmay, Chancellor of the Exchequer to Elizabeth, bought land of the Black Friars, the Dominicans, for his new college of Emmanuel. In 1594 the executors of Lady Frances Sidney, Countess of Sussex, after a lengthy wrangle, obtained from Trinity College the site of the Grey Friars, the Franciscans, for the building of Sidney Sussex College.

The 16th century established Cambridge as a University of poets. Fisher when stipulating the curriculum for Christ's College had added poetry and oratory to the traditional trivium and quadrivium, and he required the students at St John's College to present weekly copies of Greek and Latin verses. St John's was the college of Sir Thomas Wyatt, one of the first poets of the great age of English poetry to receive his education at Cambridge. If for some, Wyatt's sonnets are minor poetry, with Edmund Spenser we arrive among the poetic giants. Spenser was at Pembroke and had composed *Hymns in honour of Love and Beauty* before he came down. At St John's, Robert Greene and Thomas Nash were near contemporaries of Christopher Marlowe at Corpus Christi. He and yet another dramatist, John Fletcher, are commemorated together on a plaque in the Old Court of Corpus Christi where they both lived. Of Marlowe's life at Cambridge we know little, but his name is honoured in the Marlowe Society, a dramatic society among the founder members of which was Rupert Brooke. Nash's memories of his college were of a 'most famous and fortunate nurse of all learning' while Greene repented his misspent youth, 'Being at the University I light among wags as lewd as myself, with whom I consumed the flower of my youth.' That middle-aged smiting of his breast strikes the very modern note of the man regretting his poor degree and opportunities frittered away.

The drama developed within the colleges. In 1559 the statutes of Queens' College laid down 'Lest our youths should remain rude and unpolished in pronunciation and gesture, we will that the Greek professor shall provide

The Round Church; or Church of the Holy Sepulchre. *From a drawing by A. Brunet Debaines [c1890]*

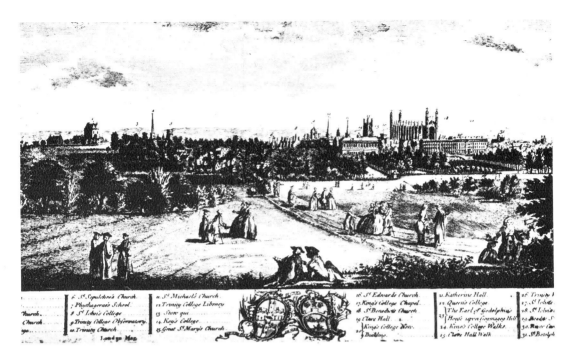

Cambridge from the North-West, 1748

for the acting in the College hall of two comedies or tragedies'.

The performance of Latin and English plays supplied a large part of the entertainment for Queen Elizabeth on her famous visit to Cambridge made between Saturday 5 August and Thursday 10 August 1564. After listening to orations in King's College chapel, and attending disputations in Great St Mary's she was regaled night after night with performances on a stage erected in the ante-chapel of King's College Chapel. On the last night of her visit she declined the offer of yet another play, explaining that she was 'over-watched with former plays'.

The students who lined the passage from Queens' College to the west end of King's College Chapel to greet the Queen would by then have been receiving more and more of their education in college. The office of tutor begins to appear in all college statutes framed in the second half of the 16th Century. Willis and Clark have given a good definition of a tutor as 'a fellow of the college who is to be responsible for his pupil's expenses, to explain to him what he has to do and to learn, and, in return, is to be treated by him with filial obedience and respect.'

As the number of tutors grew, so did the number of young gentlemen coming up to Cambridge not to become scholarly clerics, but to train themselves for their future in public life. We are at the beginning of the road that will lead us to the aristocratic prankishness of Byron who saw his tutor and the old Fellow who flanked him in his rooms in Nevile's Court as 'checks to his vivacity'.

The 17th century produced a further abundant crop of poets, nowhere more so than at Trinity. George Herbert, John Suckling, Andrew Marvell, John Dryden and Abraham Cowley were all members of Trinity. Cowley in a poem *On the death of Mr William Harvey* speaks movingly of his dead friend, a graceful homage from the poetic to the scientific tradition and at the same time a touching expression of the love that even the most prosaic of Cambridge's children must feel for her:

> Ye fields of Cambridge, our dear
>   Cambridge, say
> Have ye not seen us walking every day?
> Was there a tree about, which did not
>   know
> the love betwixt us two?

That new scientific method exemplified by

Bridge of Queens' College, looking North. *From a drawing by H. Toussaint [c1890]*

the research of men such as Harvey, a graduate of Caius, had had its great apologist in Francis Bacon, up at Trinity in the 1570's.

If Cowley recalled the natural world of Cambridge, Milton, the University's greatest poet of the 17th century, and, arguably, of any century, turned to the man made in his memories of his time at Christ's College. In *Il Penseroso* he takes us through a world of brick and stone which already felt old to a man of the 17th century.

> *But let my due feet never fail*
> *To walk the studious cloister's pale*
> *And love the high embowe'd roof,*
> *With antique pillars massy — proof,*
> *And storied windows richly dight*
> *Casting a dim religious light.*

The old fashion of building was still seen by many as the most seemly for an ancient seat of learning. When Milton came up, John's had just built a library in the gothic style. However, at Christ's, 10 years after Milton's time a new free-standing Fellows' Building in a classical mode was built. At this moment of transition from old to new the little front court at Christ's may conveniently serve to remind us of the typical college arrangement which had evolved since the first foundation at Peterhouse. We pass through a gatehouse and face across the court the oriel window of the hall. To its left is the master's lodge below which is the combination room. The master could enter the hall by a spiral staircase which connected directly with the dais. We enter the hall via the screens passage to the right of which lie the buttery, the cellars and the kitchens. In the south west corner is the library, in the north east, the college chapel. (At first the colleges did not possess their own chapels, and had to make use of the parish churches of the town.) Around the court we find the staircases off which on each floor there would be two sets of rooms. This, simply, is the pattern that is repeated, with variations in the position of the different elements, in all the medieval foundations.

In the latter part of the 17th century there was a rapid growth in the scientific study which has made Cambridge famous. In Sir Isaac Newton, Trinity possessed the greatest scientific mind of his age. He came to Cambridge in 1661, and received his first mathematical education from Dr Isaac Barrow, Master of Trinity and first Lucasian Professor of Mathematics, a chair to which

Newton succeeded. His most important work on the theory of gravitation and optics was done during his years at Cambridge, his *Principia Mathematica* being published in 1687.

Newton left Trinity in 1696 and in 1700 Richard Bentley became its Master. This distinguished classical scholar showed every encouragement to Roger Cotes, who worked on the second edition of the *Principia* and became the first Plumian Professor of Astronomy. These signs of energy in the scientific field were not evident in the classical discipline where Bentley's laudable ambition for reform was vitiated by his quarrelsome and greedy character which involved him in a long and notorious battle with his colleagues in the college and the University. That he should have wasted his opportunities was doubly sad as the University sorely needed a new beginning. As a measure of this stagnation we note that the number of matriculations declined through the 18th century and no new colleges were founded.

When the German bibliophile, von Uffenbach, visited Cambridge in 1710 he found Bentley 'as well lodged as the Queen at St James' but the condition of the books in the various college libraries that he visited was deplorable. His worst strictures were reserved for Caius College where he found the manuscripts in 'a miserable garret under the roof which could have been very little or not all all visited, for the top step was buried in pigeons' dung, and the manuscripts lay thick with dust on the floor.'

Five years after his visit in 1715, the University received a great gift of books from George I. The political colour of Cambridge was seen as the occasion for this munificence.

> The King to Oxford sent a troop of horse
> For Tories know no argument but force;
> With equal skill, to Cambridge books he sent,
> For Whigs admit no force but argument!

The consequent need for space gave the University a new building in the Senate House. With the building of the Senate House came the Senate House Examination, later to be the Mathematical Tripos. This gradually

The Senate House and University Library.
From a drawing by A. Brunet Debaines [c1890]

replaced the medieval disputations, and by 1790 examination papers were already being printed. Undergraduates prepared themselves for this examination with the help of college tutors and private coaches. This system divorced the professors from the undergraduate body and contributed to the intellectual torpor of the University.

The decadent state of the University at the end of the 18th century is paralleled in the corruption of the town. From 1788 when John Mortlock, banker, first became Mayor until 1835, his family were virtual rulers the town. His cynical disdain for those he represented is epitomised in a remark to a chess player, 'You, Sir, play with wooden men, I play with real men'. The municipal Corporation Act of 1835 put an end to their power, but it was another 15 years before a Royal Commission on the University was appointed in 1850. Change had already begun. The coming of peace which had been

Pepysian Library, Magdalene College. *From a drawing by A. Brunet Debaines [c1890]*

celebrated, albeit prematurely, in 1814 by the town's consumption of 5,338 pounds of beef and 700 plum puddings of 6lb each, had brought a rise in the number of students. Building work had begun at Downing College in 1807, the first new foundation since the 16th century. In these early years of the 19th century many of the modern undergraduate's pursuits established themselves. Debates in the Union were held at the back of the Red Lion Inn, now sadly destroyed in a shopping centre of gargantuan proportions. Literary and philosophical societies formed themselves, most noteworthy among these begin the 'Apostles' of which Tennyson was an early member. Rowing had already been confirmed as the Varsity sport par excellence. Leslie Stephen saw the 'boating man' as the 'purest type of the genuine university athlete'.

In 1825 boat clubs were founded at Trinity, which rows as 1st and 3rd, and by St John's, which acknowledges its founder and rows as LMBC — Lady Margaret Boat Club. Bumping races, now held twice a year as 'the Lents' and 'the Mays', began in 1827 and two years later the first University Boat Race took place.

> *To time thus spent, add multitudes*
> *of hours,*
> *Pilfered away by . . . Good-natured*
> *lounging.*

Wordsworth reminds us, when recalling his life at John's.

In 1847 the Royal Family once again entered the history of Cambridge when Prince Albert was elected Chancellor of the University and began to apply pressure for reform which resulted in the appointment of the Royal Commission in 1850. This along with the statutory Commission in 1877 brought about the changes necessary to lay the firm foundations for the growth of Cambridge into the vigorous University that it is today. New chairs were established, and new triposes introduced, most significantly a Natural Sciences tripos in 1851. It was the lack of adequate scientific teaching in the English universities that had been most strongly criticised from many quarters. The long list of Nobel prize winners from Cambridge is a testimony to the efficacy of those reforms. One radical change still remained to be made in the University, and that came about with the foundation by Emily Davies in 1869 of Girton College, the first college for women. A second college, Newnham, grew out of the house for women opened by Miss Clough in 1871. Cambridge's third women's college, New Hall, was founded in 1954 but since then a revolutionary change has taken place in the position of women in the university. Women are accepted as undergraduates by all the colleges with the exception, at the time of writing, of Peterhouse.

The will to create new foundations has not diminished, Selwyn College and Fitzwilliam House, now College, began life in the late

19th century. In 1958 the Senate voted for the creation of a college for 500 students and 60 fellows in honour of Sir Winston Churchill. This ambitious project has been housed in buildings which while modern in form have respected the courtyard pattern of the traditional Cambridge college. The eponymous founder of Robinson College takes a direct and personal interest in his benefaction in the manner of the royal and aristocratic founders and foundresses of the Middle Ages. The old colleges have scattered new courts and hostels across the Cambridge landscape so that today Cambridge can serve as an extended exhibition of the development of architectural styles over the last 20 years. Change comes at Cambridge against a backdrop of permanence. The image of the Backs and King's College Chapel imprinted on the mind of any lover of Cambridge remains happily immutable.

Cambridge looks forward with optimism. That close collaboration between Universities and Industry so strongly advocated by all governments has found physical shape here in the number of high technology companies that ring Cambridge. A city of the future living in medieval courts, its denizens like Wordsworth's Newton, *Voyaging through strange seas of thought*. The astronomers who work at the university radio telescope stretching five kilometers long beside the Barton Road appreciate the irony. The radio signals come to them from stars that may have died before those first students arrived from Oxford in 1209.

South Porch of King's College Chapel. *From a drawing by A. Brunet Debaines [c1890]*

INTRODUCTION

EINLEITUNG

Les Romains fondèrent "Grantchester" en l'an 70 après J.C., sur les rives d'un cours d'eau qu'ils appelèrent "Granta". Mais à l'époque des Anglo-Saxons son nom dentnt "Grantabridge", que les Normands transformérent en "Cambridge" après 1066; certaines parties de la rivière Cem sont encore appelées "Granta".

Le premier collège, Peterhouse, fut fondé en 1284. Au cours des XIV. et XV. siècles, l'Université se développa rapidement. Neuf nouveaux collèges furent construits, y compris le célèbre King's Collège, fondé par le jeune roi Henri VI en 1441 pour aller de pair avec son nouveau collège d'Eton pour les garçons plus jeunes. Les collèges ne furent pas tous fondés par la royauté. Certains furent établis par des évêques — Trinity Hall (1350) par exemple. D'autres furent fondés par des membres de riches familles, comme la Comtesse de Pembroke, dont le collège fut commencé en 1347. D'autres encore furent créés par des milieux commerciaux — le premier fut Corpus Christi, fondé en 1352 par une corporation urbaine. Au cours des siècles qui suivirent, d'autres collèges furent construits et certains des plus anciens furent agrandis. Il existait une vaste gamme de parrains: certains étaient royaux, d'autres épiscopaux, de nombreux autres des gens riches de l'époque.

Ceci explique la variété magnifique des styles d'architecture anglaise que l'on peut voir à Cambridge, où le gothique du Moyen-Age voisine avec le baroque Géorgien et les créations plus fonctionnelles du XX. siècle, telles que New Hall (1954), Churchill College (1959) et le plus récent collège, fondé grâce à la générosité d'un homme d'affaires de Cambridge, Robinson College (1980).

Mais Cambridge, malgré les anciennes bâtisses qui l'ont rendue célèbre dans le Monde entier, est l'une des villes les plus modernes de l'Angleterre. Une étroite collaboration entre l'Université et l'industrie s'est traduite physiquement par le grand nombre de sociétés de haute technologie ceinturant la ville — une cité de l'avenir vivant dans des cours médiévales.

Die Römer gründeten "Grantchester" an einem Fluß, den sie im Jahre 70 A.D. die Granta nannten. Zur Zeit der Angelsachsen hatte sich der Stadtname in "Grantabridge" verwandelt, und dieser wurde dann von den Normannen bald nach 1066 in "Cambridge" abgeändert, aber streckenweise wird der Fluß auch heute noch die "Granta" genannt. Peterhouse, das erste College, wurde 1284 gegründet. Während des 14. und des 15. Jahrhunderts weitete sich die Universität rasch aus. Es wurden neun neue Colleges gegründet, darunter das berühmte King's College des jungen Königs Heinrich dem Sechsten, der es 1441 stiftete, als Gegenstück zu seinem neuen Eton College für jüngere Knaben. Nicht alle Colleges wurden vom Königshaus gegründet. Einige wurden von Bischöfen gestiftet — Trinity Hall (1350) mag als Beispiel dienen. Andere wiederum wurden von Angehörigen reicher Familien gegründet, wie der Gräfin von Pembroke, zu deren College der Grundstein 1347 gelegt wurde. Wieder andere Colleges verdanken ihren Ursprung Handelsinteressen — das erste davon war das Corpus Christi College, das 1352 von der Stadtgilde gegründet wurde. In den folgenden Jahrhunderten wurden weitere Colleges gestiftet und bereits bestehende erweitert. Die Geldgeber kamen aus den verschiedensten Kreisen: manche gehörten zur königlichen Familie, andere waren Bischöfe, viele jedoch waren die jeweils reichsten Bürger ihrer Zeit. Daraus erklärt sich die wunderbare Vielfalt der englischen architektonischen Stile, die heute in Cambridge zu sehen sind. Seite an Seite stehen Bauten mittelalterlicher Gotik, solche des georgianischen Barocks und die mehr als Zweckbauten konzipierten Schöpfungen des 20. Jahrhunderts, wie etwa das New Hall (1954), das Churchill College (1959) und das erst jüngst erbaute Robinson College (. . .), das seinen Ursprung der Großzügigkeit eines Geschäftsmannes aus Cambridge verdankt. Dennoch ist Cambridge, all seinen alten Gebäuden zum Trotz und auch wenn es durch diese weltberühmt geworden ist, eine von Englands modernsten Städten. Die enge Zusammenarbeit zwischen der Universität und der Industrie hat sich konkret in einer Anzahl von Industriewerken, die sich rund um die Stadt angesiedelt haben, niedergeschlagen. So ist denn Cambridge die Stadt der Zukunft, trotz seiner mittelalterlichen Höfe.

紹　介

カメラカラー・カメオ：ケンブリッジ

紀元前70年に、ローマ人がグランタという川に沿ってグラントチェスターという町を作りました。その名はアングロ・サクソン時代にグランタブリッジとかえられ、それはまた、1066年の後、ノルマン人によってケンブリッジとかえられました。しかし、カム川の近辺では今だにグランタと呼んでいます。

ピーターハウスという最初のカレッジは、1284年に創設され、14世紀～15世紀にかけて急速に拡大しました。若い男子学生のための新しいイートン・カレッジの相対校として1441年に若いヘンリー6世によって創設された有名なキングス・カレッジを含め、9校の新しいカレッジが創設されました。王室が全カレッジを設立したわけではありません。例えば、トリニティー・ホール（1350年）のように主教が設立したものもあります。

他には、1347年に開校したカレッジで、ペンブロック伯爵夫人のような富豪一家のメンバーにより設立されたものもあります。又、更に、商業界によって設立されたもの、例えば先ず、1352年に最初に町のギルドによって設立されたコーパス・クリスティ・カレッジがあります。次の世紀に入っても更にカレッジは設立され、そして古いカレッジは拡大されていきました。カレッジ設立においては様々なスポンサーがおり、いくつかは王室が、または教会が、そしてまた、当時の多くの金持の市民といった人達でした。これは、ケンブリッジで見られる非常に様々な英国風建築類で詳細に説明しています。これは、中世期のゴシック建築はジョージ王朝期のバロック様式に並び、そしてニュー・ホール（1954年）、チャーチル・カレッジ（1959年）、そして最も最近、ケンブリッジの寛大なビジネスマンによって設立されたロビンソン・カレッジのように、20世紀の最も実用的に設立されたものもあります。

しかし、ケンブリッジは、古い建物のたちならぶ町として世界中に有名にもかかわらず、英国の最も近代的な町の一つでもあります。

カレッジと企業との密接な協力が、ハイ・テクノロジーの数々の会社といったケンブリッジの町を囲む中世期の広場で生活している未来の町という具体的な形を造りあげています。

View from Great St Mary's
Cambridge does not offer the
visitor an abundance of
viewpoints from which to survey
the beauties of the city, but from
the tower of Great St Mary's one
can look out over towers and
roofs and begin to make some
sense of what, on the ground,
appears to be a maze of streets,
passages, lanes, courts and
gateways. Here we look north
west from the tower. In the
foreground we almost seem to be
able to touch the pinnacles of the
flamboyant Frenchified tower of
Alfred Waterhouse's building of
1870 for the Tree Court of
Gonville and Caius College.

Beyond, our attention is
immediately caught by the Great
Court of Trinity College, a fine
expanse of grass in this dense
cluster of buildings. On its
northern edge lies the long
regular shape of the 16th century
Chapel abutting at its west end
King Edward's Tower of 1428-
32.

Between us and the Chapel
rises the broad brick built mass of
Great Gate, first referred to in
1528-9. Behind the east end of
the Chapel the gatehouse of
St John's College built from
1511-20, completes this trio of
examples of one of Cambridge's
most characteristic building
forms.

Above the earlier buildings the
great square tower of St John's
College dominates our view. Built
by Sir George Gilbert Scott in
1863-69 it too draws inspiration
from France in its high roofed
form. It has taken its place as one
of the landmarks of the
Cambridge skyline. It and King's
Chapel and the tower of
University Library vie for the
attention of the approaching
traveller eager for the first
glimpse of Cambridge.

Panorama vu de la tour de l'église
Great St. Mary.

Blick vom Turm der Kirche Great
St. Mary

グレート・セント・メリーの教会の塔
からの眺め

The Fitzwilliam Museum, Trumpington Street The Fitzwilliam Museum's grand portico of eight Corinthian columns stands on Trumpington Street between Scroope Terrace and the buildings of Peterhouse.

Richard, Viscount Fitzwilliam, died in 1816, having bequeathed to the University his collection of paintings and etchings, his library and £100,000 stock to finance the building, staffing and future purchases of the foundation. For more than 30 years the collection was housed in other buildings until 1848 it moved into its still uncompleted home. This was designed by George Basevi but the work was carried on after his death by C. R. Cockerell and Edward Barry.

Beyond the portico lies a richly decorated entrance hall and ornate marble staircase leading to the main picture galleries. Here the composity of the Museum's welcome gives way to an airy and leisurely spaciousness in galleries predominantly lit by natural light where oriental rugs and good furniture set off the paintings.

Fitzwilliam's original bequest included works by Titian, Veronese and Rembrandt. Later gifts and purchases have brought paintings of all schools. It has a particularly fine print room and a magnificent cabinet of coins and medals the nucleus of which is the collection of Dr Andrew Perne given to the University in 1589. It also boasts Greek, Roman, and Egyptian antiquities, one of the best collections of pottery and porcelain in Britain and a department of arms and armour and textiles.

Le musée Fitzwilliam, fondé en 1816, contient un grand nombre de fameux tableaux, dont des oeuvres de Titian, Veronese et Rembrandt.

Das 1816 gegründete Fitzwilliam-Museum, in dem sich viele berühmte Gemälde befinden, darunter Gemälde von Tizian, Veronese und Rembrandt.

ティツィアーノ、ベロネーゼ、および
レンブラントの作品など数々の有名な
絵画のある1816年に設立されたフィッ
ツウイリアム美術館

Peterhouse Peterhouse displays itself with an open stylishness behind noble wrought iron railings and stone gateways of 1751 and gives little hint to the casual observer that it is the oldest collegiate foundation in Cambridge.

In 1280 Hugh de Balsham, Bishop of Ely, founded a college in the Hospital of St John, but the scholars met with opposition from the regular canons and moved to the present site in 1284. The Hall and Buttery retain parts dating from 1290. Sadly the principal court was largely modernised in 1754 to conform with the regularity of 18th century taste and the Hall itself was refaced in 1870. Thus the oldest college buildings in Cambridge were robbed of their air of antiquity.

At first the college had no chapel and used the adjoining church of Little St Mary's. The college chapel that now faces Trumpington Street is a playful essay of 1628/32 built under the Mastership of Matthew Wren, Bishop of Ely and uncle of the architect.

To the left of the chapel the Library Range projects to the line of the street. Begun in 1590 and extended in 1633 it contains the library of Dr Andrew Perne, Master of the College from 1554 to 1580 Vice Chancellor of the University, and a great collector of books and coins. His reputation has suffered because of the skill with which he changed his convictions in order to navigate the dark and dangerous waters of religious controversy in the 16th century. University wags no longer said that a cloak had been turned, but that it had been 'Perned'!

Peterhouse, le collège le plus ancien, se dresse derrière des grilles et portes cochères construites en 1751.

Peterhouse, das älteste College, das hinter einer Einfriedung und einem Tor steht, die 1751 erbaut wurden.

1751年に設けられた鉄柵と門の後にある最も古いカレッジのピーターハウス

Pembroke College: Gateway On Christmas Eve 1347 Mary de St Pol, Countess of Pembroke, widow of Aymer de Valence, founded her college. A woman of great wealth she devoted herself to good works after her husband's untimely death — the sad tradition that he was killed on their wedding day is apocryphal. Her attraction to the teachings of St Francis prompted her to adopt the curious arrangement of appointing two external rectors, one of them a Franciscan.

The original foundation had only one court, the smallest in Cambridge, and this disappeared in the Victorian need for expansion. However the gateway remains as the only example of a fourteenth century college entrance. The two oriel windows, although refaced in the 18th century, date from that first building. In contrast to the mighty gatehouses of other colleges, Pembroke guards itself against the outside world with a quiet domestic dignity. The college provided Christopher Wren with his first architectural commission and Cambridge with its first truly classical building. His uncle, Matthew Wren, Bishop of Ely, formerly Master of Peterhouse, had passed the years between 1642 and 1659 in the Tower and was lucky to have escaped the fate of Archbishop Laud. As a thank-offering for his release he presented £5,000 and commissioned his nephew to design a chapel for his old college of Pembroke.

Le porche d'entrée de Pembroke College est le seul exemple d'une entrée de collège du XIV. siècle.

Das Tor zum Pembroke College, das einzige Beispiel eines College-Eingangs aus dem 14. Jahrhundert.

14世紀のカレッジの入口のもので唯一つ残されたペンブロック・カレッジの門

The Pitt Press and Trumpington Street King's Parade becomes Trumpington Street where Silver Street enters from the west. The Pitt Press stands beyond the junction. The tall oriel window included in the design of 1831 by Blore was to light the room set aside for meetings of the Press Syndicate.

Printing had come to Cambridge in 1521 when the German John Siberch produced his first book in Cambridge, the *Oratio* of Henry Bullock in honour of Cardinal Wolsey's visit. Henry VIII granted the university a charter but actual printing activity was desultory and the London printers did everything in their power to prevent the growth of this rival. However in the early 17th century many famous books were printed including William Harvey's treatise *De Circulatione Sanguinis* (on the Circulation of the Blood) in 1649. Bibles and prayer books remained the staple of the Press, but forays into more speculative publishing ventures revealed the shortcomings of academics as men of business and in 1737 a Syndicate was appointed to take matters in hand.

The present building was the gift of the Pitt Memorial Committee who found that they had to hand £10,700 needed for this job after paying for the statue of Pitt in Hanover Square. This and the University Pitt Club in Jesus Lane are the two Cambridge memories to the great statesman William Pitt, the younger, who had been a Pembroke man.

Pitt Press est le siège original de la maison d'imprimerie et d'édition de l'Université créée en 1521.

Die Pitt-Druckerei ist die ursprüngliche Heimstätte der Universitätsdruckerei und des Universitätsverlages, die beide 1521 gegründet wurden.

ピット・プレスという名称は、1521 年に設立したユニバシティー印刷および発行社の本来の名称です

President's Gallery, Queens'
Cambridge, in a region not
blessed by abundant building
stone, cannot boast medieval
cloisters enlivened by carving of
the quality found at Oxford. Here
in the Cloister Court of Queens'
College we find instead a
charming domesticity. There is no
grand formality either in the
architecture or in the cottage
garden quality of the planting.

Queens' shares with King's the
distinction of not having a
Master. King's places a Provost
at its head and Queens' is
governed by a President. Here we
look north across the court at the
16th century President's gallery
which runs at right angles to the
President's Lodge built in the
15th Century.

Both in this court and in its
Front Court, Queens' College
displays to the curious tourist the
most complete group of college
buildings from the Middle Ages.
We enter the college by the
Gatehouse of 1448 and in the rib
vault above us we can pick out
two bosses representing
St Margaret and St Bernard. Two
saints intimately connected with
the story of the founding of the
college. Andrew Dockett,
Principal of St Bernard's Hostel
obtained a royal charter to found
a college from Henry VI in 1446
but within two years this charter
had been surrendered and a new
one granted by Henry to his wife
Margaret of Anjou who was no
doubt anxious to emulate her
husband's great benefaction at
King's College.

La Galerie du Président de
Queen's College fut construite
durant le XVI. siècle, à angle droit
avec la Loge du Président.

Die Rektorgallerie im Queen's
College wurde im 16.
Jahrhundert erbaut und verläuft
im rechten Winkel zum Rektorat.

クイーンズ・カレッジのプレジデンツ
・ギャラリーは、16世紀に建てられ、
それはプレジデンツ・ロッジと直角に
位置しています

26

Queens' College: Mathematical Bridge From Silver Street bridge we look north up the Cam at punts approaching the turning point in their tour, unless their occupants are willing to haul them over the rollers into the Granta. They pass beneath the brick walls of Queen's College and its Mathematical Bridge.

The bridge was built in 1749 by James Essex following designs of William Etheridge which allowed the individual members to be pegged together without the use of any nails.

The bridge connects the old courts to college land west of the river, formerly occupied only by the Brewhouse and the Fellows' fruit garden. In this century it has been made the site of two new buildings, the first of which commemorates that great scholar and President of Queens', John Fisher.

Fisher was elected President in 1505 at a moment when he had been charged by Lady Margaret Beaufort with the supervision of her first Cambridge foundation, Christ's College. He resigned in 1508 because his duties prevented him from residing. These duties were later to include the carrying to a successful conclusion of Lady Margaret's plan for her second college, John's.

Fisher's friend, Erasmus, the great Dutch humanist, lived at Queens' from 1511 to 1514.

Les charpentes du Mathematical Bridge enjambant la Cam furent chevillées sans l'aide de clous. Il fut construit en 1749.

Das Holzgerippe der "Mathematical Bridge" (Mathematischen Brücke) über den Cam wurde ohne Verwendung von Nägeln zusammengefügt. Die Brücke wurde 1749 errichtet.

カム川に渡るマテ ィマテ ィカル・ブリ ッジの大木は、鉄くぎを使用せず、木 くぎを使っており、1749年に建造され たものです

King's Parade On 12 February 1441, King Henry VI issued letters patent for the foundation of a college to consist of a Rector and 12 students. These original modest proposals were soon abandoned and in 1443 Henry established a strong and permanent bond between King's College and his foundation of 1440, Eton College. William of Wykeham's twin foundations of Winchester College and New College, Oxford had provided him with the example of such a link and Henry's ambition was to emulate it on a royal scale.

When he laid the first stone of the chapel on St James' Day, 25 July 1446, the number of scholars contemplated had risen to 70. In 1448, he wrote his 'Will' — not a testament, but a memorandum giving in great detail his vision of the completed college and entrusting the direction of operations to William Waynfleet, Bishop of Winchester.

Henry saw his college as a great enclosure protected from the town and the rest of the University by high walls reminiscent of the monastery or the castle. The land was bought and a huge tract in the centre of medieval Cambridge was removed from the use of the townspeople. Building work began on the chapel at last under the master mason Reginald of Ely, but was broken off at Henry's capture in 1461. Some work began again in 1476 and Edward IV's gift of 1480 allowed more substantial activity. Henry VII, that princely administrator lacked the holy fervour of his uncle, but gave three great donations the last of them in his will. These ensured the completion of the Chapel by 1515.

Les réfectoire, bibliothèque et écran du King's College furent construits en 1824/8.

Der Speisesaal, die Bibliothek und die Trennwand im King's College wurden 1824-28 erbaut.

キングス・カレッジのホール、図書館、およびスクリーンは1824年〜1828年に建てられました

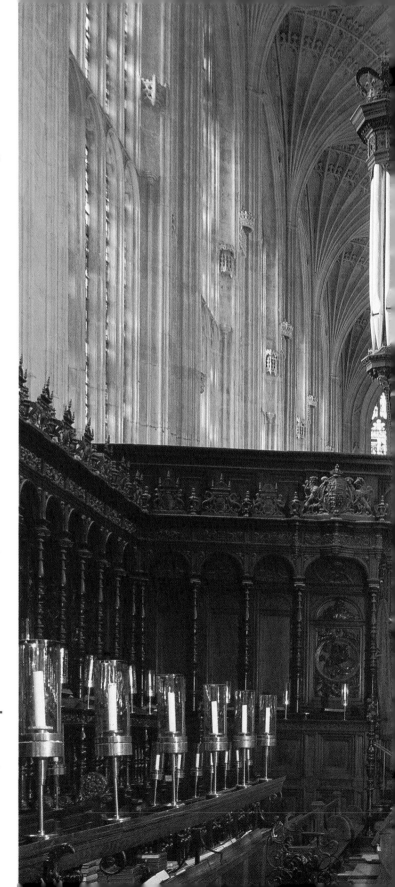

King's College Chapel Interior
Inside King's College Chapel as
we look back from the Choir we
forget any sense of a grand
design uncompleted. The interior
of this crowning achievement of
the Perpendicular style follows
with glorious effect the founder's
wishes that the building of his
college should be 'In large fourme
clene and substantial, settyng a
parte superfluite of too great
curious works of enteille and
besy moulding'.

The great fan fault was not
originally contemplated but in its
noble clarity it satisfied Henry's
specifications in a way that a
more intricate lierne vault might
not have done. Wordsworth
looked up at 'that branching roof
scooped into ten thousand
cells . . . where music dwells
lingering'.

The musical tradition of King's
was foreseen from the very
beginning when the choir stalls
and screen were carved by
French or Italian craftsmen. They
date from 1530-5 as the cypher
of Anne Boleyn bears witness.
The organ, the oldest in
Cambridge dates in part from
1605, to fill this choir the college
maintains a choir school and
provides choral scholarships for
undergraduates. The service of
carols at King's is broadcast
every year and has become for
many people an essential part of
the celebration of Christmas.

The rich dark wood of the
stalls and the austere stone of the
vault is balanced by a joyous
panoply of colours in the stained
glass windows. Begun in 1515
by Bernard Flower, Henry VIII's
own glazier, they were completed
over the next 15 years by his and
other German, Netherlandish and
English hands. They rank among
the finest series in England and
still follow the medieval pattern
that pointed parallels between
the Old and New Testaments.

L'intérieur de la chapelle du
King's College, achevée en 1515.

Innenansicht der 1515
fertiggestellten Kapelle im King's
College.

1515年に完成したキングス・カレッ
ジ教会の内装

Clare College: Bridge The bridge at Clare College we know was built by Thomas Grumbold, mason, in 1639-40. He was paid three shillings for the drawing, but whether he actually designed this most beautiful of the Cambridge bridges we may doubt. The college was well pleased with his work and his son Robert Grumbold was master mason of the stately west front of the college that we see beyond the bridge. This delightful prospect is framed for us by the tracery of the wrought iron gate. This delicate triumph of the ironworker's art stands at the entrance to Clare Fellows' Garden. Made by Warren it is the second of the three gates by his hand that we must pass as we go east to west through the court and garden of the college. A raised path leads us through the Fellows' Garden which lies below us on either side of the third gate which closes off the college grounds from the common land beyond. The college account books record; 'Warren (blacksmith) 6 March 1713 and 7 May 1714 in full for the iron gate next the fields . . . £35.0s 0d.'

The very compactness of the well ordered beauty of Clare and its garden meant that after World War 1 it had to build its Memorial Court on the far side of the Queens' road. This move has been followed by other colleges in need of space, but the westward expansion of the colleges has not impinged upon the Backs which have remained sacrosanct.

Le pont de Clare College fut construit en 1639/40 et les portés forgées datent de 1714.

Die Brücke am Clare College wurde 1639-40 erbaut, die schmiedeeisernen Tore im Jahre 1714.

クレア・カレッジにある橋は1639年〜1640年に建てられましたが、その錬鉄の門は1714年に建造されたものです

Clare College: entrance
Opposite the entrance to the Old Court of King's at the end of Trinity Lane stands Clare College, behind fine wrought iron gates, one of a set of three made for the college by Warren. Built, apart from the Chapel, over the course of 77 years beginning in 1638, it presents a more uniform stylistic appearance than any other college before the new foundations of the 19th and 20th centuries.

John Evelyn, visiting Cambridge in 1654, noted 'Clare is of a new and noble designe, but not finish'd'. This newness conceals from us the fact that this is the second oldest collegiate foundation in Cambridge.

It had been founded as University Hall in 1326, but was refounded in 1338 by Elizabeth de Burgh, youngest daughter of Gilbert, Earl of Clare and Joan of Acre, daughter of Edward I. Thus Clare can lay claim to being the first college to have a royal connection. Of equal importance was Lady Clare's desire to bring poor but able boys to the University, and to form a community which included undergraduates as well as a Master, fellows and graduates. Here at Clare this type of college appeared at Cambridge for the first time antedating its introduction at New College, Oxford by some 40 years.

L'entrée de Clare College, fondé par Lady Clare en 1338.

Der Eingang zum Clare College, das von Lady Clare 1338 gestiftet wurde.

1338年にレイディー・クレアが設立したクレア・カレッジの入口

Trinity Hall   In Trinity Lane we come to Trinity Hall a college separated by Garret Hostel Lane from its far larger, but younger, neighbour Trinity College. Trinity Hall is an example of a college founded with a specific educational purpose, in its case the training of lawyers. The medieval church had to administer a complicated bureaucracy and legal system and the king needed lawyers for his civil and diplomatic service. Both groups of men would naturally be clergy and in 1350 William Bateman, Bishop of Norwich, determined to establish the College of the Scholars of the Holy Trinity of Norwich as a perpetual College of Scholars of the Canon and Civil Law. The study of canon law lapsed with the Reformation and the College concentrated on the study of civil law. From 1666 to 1873 two Masters and 10 Fellows of Trinity Hall held the Regius Professorship of Civil Law.

Trinity Hall has always been closely confined by its neighbours. The wealth of a royal foundation such as King's prevented its buying land west of the river and thus Trinity Hall alone of the colleges with a river frontage between Magdalen Bridge and Silver Street Bridge has no garden or buildings across the Cam. It has however created a garden within its restricted precincts which Henry James — a most capable judge — pronounced to be unsurpassed in Europe. The Library is housed in the brick building of Elizabeth's reign that we see here.

Trinity Hall fut fondé en 1350 par l'évêque de Norwich pour la formation d'hommes de lois.

Trinity Hall wurde 1350 vom Bischof von Norwich zur Ausbildung von Rechtsanwälten gegründet.

弁護士の教育のためにノリッチの主教が1350年に設立したトリニティー・ホール

Gate of Honour, Caius College
We stand behind the railings by the former University Library — now the Squire Law Library — and look across Senate House Passage at the Gate of Honour and to the right the Gate of Virtue of Gonville and Caius College.

Gonville Hall had been founded in 1348 by Edmund Gonville of Norfolk, but it might have failed three years later on the founder's death if William Bateman, Bishop of Norwich, and founder of neighbouring Trinity Hall, had not accomplished the project.

About 170 years later its third founder, John Keys of Norwich, came to the college as a young scholar. In 1539 equipped with a Fellowship and the Latinised name of Caius he set out for Padua to study medicine with the famous Vesalius. He returned in 1544 and rose quickly in his profession to become physician successively to Edward VI and Queen Mary, and finally President of the College of Physicians.

He had brought back from his travels not only new medical knowledge but also Renaissance ideals of philosophy and architecture. These he put into practice when in 1557 he refounded his old college. He devised a plan that would be instructive, decorative and healthy. The physical lay-out of the college was to set forth the moral and intellectual path that the diligent student would have to follow before he could achieve the Doctorate that was his goal.

Caius College (prononcé "Keys" en anglais) fut fondé en 1557 par un étudiant de Cambridge devenu médecin royal.

Caius (wird wie Keis ausgesprochen) College wurde 1557 von einem ehemaligen Studenten der Universität Cambridge, der später königlicher Leibarzt wurde, gestiftet.

キーズ・カレッジは、後に王室の医師となったケンブリッジ卒の生徒によって1557年に設立されたものです

Senate House   The University had built a regent house on part of the Old Schools in 1400, but many University ceremonies had to take place in Great St Mary's. Various plans for improvement had been put forward. In 1713/14 Nicholas Hawksmoor had produced a grandiose plan for a baroque centre to Cambridge but nothing had been built.

The need for a new building was made more urgent in 1715 when King George I at the instigation of Lord Townsend, presented to the University the library of John Moore, Bishop of Ely, who had died in 1714. It doubled the size of the University's collection which was already taking up more and more space in the Old Schools. A new Regent house or Senate house had to be built and in 1722 James Gibbs submitted a plan for a quadrangle open to the east, containing a new Royal Library, a Registry, Consistory and Printing House, and a Senate House. This last was the only part of the plan to be carried out.

Gibbs' design provides not only a dignified meeting place for the governing body of the University but also an elegant setting for the final act of the undergraduate's career. It is on these lovingly tended lawns that he will stand in his gown and academic hood, mortar board clutched awkwardly, surrounded by admiring relations on the day when he receives his degree.

Les étudiants reçoivent leurs deplômes dans le Maison du Sénat (Senate House) à la fin de leur carrière universitaire.

Studenten erhalten nach Studienabschluss ihre akademischen Grade im Senatshaus.

学生は、卒業式にはセネタ・ハウスで
学位を受けます

The Market Hill Throughout its history Cambridge has been a centre of communication and trade. Here on Market Hill — Cambridge, being in a part of the country poorly endowed with hills has developed the habit of calling apparently flat surfaces hills — there is a daily market. It is much like any other in a reasonably large town apart from the fact that it is dominated by two large medieval churches. The University Church of Great St Mary's and King's College Chapel. The first church of Great St Mary's dates from 1205 and the present church from the 15th century. Great St Mary's has served many purposes besides the strictly religious. It housed the University Chest, disputations were held here and degrees conferred until the building of the Senate House in the 18th century. Conferences between the University and townspeople took place here. In 1381, in one of the all too frequent clashes between 'town' and 'gown', the charters and other deeds were taken from the church and burnt on Market Hill much to the delight of one old woman who cried 'Away with the learning of the clerks! Away with it'.

The present broad, well-built church in the best tradition of East Anglian architecture was begun in 1478 and its tower took more than a century to complete. The corner turrets were finished in 1608 and the churchwarden, John Warren, died in an accident, a sad event recorded in an inscription on the tower:

Here John Warren sleeps
among the dead,
Who with the church
his own life finished.

Market Hill est un centre commercial pour Cambridge et ses environs depuis un grand nombre de siècles.

Der Market Hill (Markthügel) ist seit Jahrhunderten ein Handelszentrum für Cambridge und seine Umgebung.

マーケット・ヒルは、数世紀にわたりケンブリッジおよびその周辺のトレードの中心地となってきました

Trinity College, Great Court The Great Court of Trinity College is the largest college court at either Oxford or Cambridge. In 1546 Henry VIII founded Trinity College 'to the glory of God and advantage of the realm, for the promotion of science, philosophy, liberal arts and theology'. Great Court covers the site of three earlier foundations, King's Hall, Physick Hostel, and Michaelhouse.

King's Hall was created a college by Edward III in 1337 and had had fellows and undergraduates known as the King's Childer. Michaelhouse, founded in 1324 by Hervey de Stanton, Chancellor of the Exchequer to Edward II, was reserved for clerics and was thus dissolved in 1546 at which point Henry took the decision to refound King's Hall.

The entrance gate of King's Hall was built in 1428/32 but was moved in 1599/1600 to its present position at the west end of Trinity Chapel. The Chapel itself, long and low in its proportions had been built in 1555-1567, by the Master, Dr Thomas Nevile. Under the clock a statute of Edward III stares across the Court at the Fountain built 1601-5. Not set in the dead centre of a court which is itself asymmetrical, the fountain provides a gentle sound of splashing water as an accompaniment to the lucubrations or libations of the fellows and undergraduates fortunate enough to live on one of the staircases of Great Court.

Trinity College, construit par Henri VIII à partir de 1546, est la plus grande cour universitaire en Angleterre.

Der Hof des Trinity College, dessen Bau König Heinrich der Achte im Jahre 1546 in Angriff nahm. Er ist der größte Universitätshof Englands.

1546年からヘンリー8世に建てられたトリニティー・カレッジ・コートは英国の大学で最も大きいコートです

Trinity College Hall Dr Thomas Nevile who became Master of Trinity in 1593 was a man of means. He lent the college £3,000 on easy terms and immediately began a building programme that would give the new college those elements of the collegiate plan that it still lacked. Chief among these was a hall of sufficient dignity.

The hall is the centre of the life of any college. Here the master and the fellows and undergraduates, the senior and junior members of the college should eat dinner together however widely their paths may diverge during the rest of the day.

Behind the High Table Henry VIII, in a portrait by Hans Eworth, surveys the inheritors of his foundation. The Royal coat of arms surrounded by exuberant Jacobean strapwork proudly proclaims the Royal connection while the display of heraldic glass, gives us a colourful catalogue of some of the great and worthy names of member's' of Trinity.

The hall is covered by a hammerbeam roof and is entered by undergraduates through a magnificent screen with a gallery over. The screen conceals the passage off which we find the Buttery and the kitchens where either by design or accident that Trinity speciality, Creme Brulee, was invented. The fellows enter through the doors behind the High Table which will lead them back after dinner to the Fellow's Parlour and Cambination Room, and the delights of port and good conversation. Beyond is the Master's Lodge completed by Thomas Nevile in 1600 which apart from housing the Master provides lodging for the Judge conducting the Assizes.

Le réfectoire de Trinity College où les maître et confrères, ainsi que les étudiants, prennent leur repas ensemble.

Der Speisesaal des Trinity College, wo der Rektor, die Professoren und die Studenten gemeinsam speisen.

学寮長、特別研究員および学生が共に食事をするトリニティ イー・カレッジ・ホール

Trinity, Wren Library In 1675, Dr Isaac Barrow, the Master of Trinity, urged the University to erect a building where speeches could be made in dignified surroundings (thus avoiding the scandal of deforming the University Church with scaffolds and defiling it with rude crowds and outcries). His proposal was turned down, and out of pique at the pusillanimity of his colleagues he decided to plan for his own college something 'more magnificent and costly'.

As architect he chose Christopher Wren who had in 1663 designed his first work of architecture, the Sheldonian Theatre at Oxford, a building intended to serve just that purpose which Barrow's contemporaries felt they could neglect.

Wren placed his building west of the wall of Nevile's Court facing the river, although the colonnades of the court were later extended to join up with the library. He gave Barrow an edifice impressive in its stern grandeur. Inside, Wren adopted a new arrangement for the bookcases which would allow them to stretch along the walls without interruption as well as to project into the body of the room. This he achieved by lowering the floor level so that the tops of the bookcases came below the line of the windows.

The bookcases themselves were embellished by Grinling Gibbons with what Celia Fiennes, a 17th century visitor, called 'the finest carving in wood in flowers, birds, leaves, figures of all sorts, as ever I saw'.

La bibliothèque de Trinity College fut conçue par Sir Christopher Wren, l'architecte de la cathédrale St. Paul, en 1675.

Die Bibliothek des Trinity College, die von Sir Christopher Wren, dem Architekten der Paulskathedrale, 1675 entworfen wurde.

セント・ポール寺院の建築家、サー・クリストファー・レンによって1675年に設計されたトリニティー・カレッジ図書館

John's Gatehouse Out of Bridge Street sweeps St John's Street which with Trinity Street formed the original High Street. We look across from the churchyard of the now demolished All Saints at the great brick gatehouse of St John's College and a scatter of bicycles against the neat chains in front of the well worn brick walls. The gaudily emblazoned arms above the archway are those of Lady Margaret Beaufort, mother of Henry VII and foundress of this and Christ's College. Both her foundations are distinguished by these magnificent entrances, that at Christ's being in stone. Here at John's the daisies strewn across the ground of the carving were the particular emblem of Lady Margaret.

Lady Margaret died in 1509 and thus did not live to see the final dissolution of St John's College in 1511 as provided in her will. It was John Fisher, her chaplain and her helper in her earlier foundation at Christ's, who ensured that her scheme came to fruition. 800,000 bricks had been ordered even before the last inhabitants of the hospital had left for Ely, and the college was opened in 1516 although building continued until 1520.

Behind the gate lie three axially aligned courts which apart from the intrusion of Gilbert Scott's Chapel on the north side of the first court form a remarkably homogeneous group. John's now ranks second to Trinity in number of undergraduates but for many years it was the largest college and this need for accommodation dictated the building of a whole succession of courts.

La loge à l'entrée de St. John's College porte les armoiries de sa fondatrice, Lady Margaret Beaufort, la mère du roi Henri VII.

Das Pförtnerhaus des St. John's College trägt das Wappen seiner Stifterin, der Lady Margaret Beaufort, der Mutter Heinrichs des Siebten.

セント・ジョンズ・カレッジの門番詰所は、その設立者であるヘンリー7世の母君、レイディー・マーガレット・ボーフォートの紋が刻まれています

John's Library and the Bridge of Sighs From the corner of the New Court of John's we look back at the window of the Library and the famous Bridge of Sighs. Nowhere in Cambridge can the attachment to the Gothic style as the true and fitting style for an ancient University be seen more clearly. JLCS the initials above the window proudly proclaim the name of Johnannes Lincolniensis *Custos Sigilli*, that is Bishop Williams of Lincoln, Lord Keeper of the Great Seal and the donator of money for the Library. The great oriel window had originally been disliked by this benefactor, but he had been persuaded by his fellow Bishop Carey of Exeter, who told him 'that some men of judgement like the best the old fashion of church window, holding it most meet for such a building'.

The college had contented itself with its expansion to the east bank of the river until the early 19th century. Then in 1827-31 the New Court was erected to the designs of Thomas Rickman and Henry Hutchinson. Hutchinson built the delightfully graceful Bridge of Sighs, a much lighter and more playful structure than its namesake in Venice. The sighs here are occasioned by the iron bars placed across the arches to prevent late and intrepid undergraduates from entering the college by this route.

Le pont reliant les cours neuves et anciennes de St. John's College est connu sous le nom de "Pont des Soupirs".

Die Brücke, die den neuen mit dem alten Hof des St. John's College verbindet, ist unter dem Namen der "Seufzerbrücke" bekannt geworden.

セント・ジョンズ・カレッジの新しいコートと古いコートにかかる橋は、ブリッジ・オブ・サイ、「ためいきの橋」として知られています

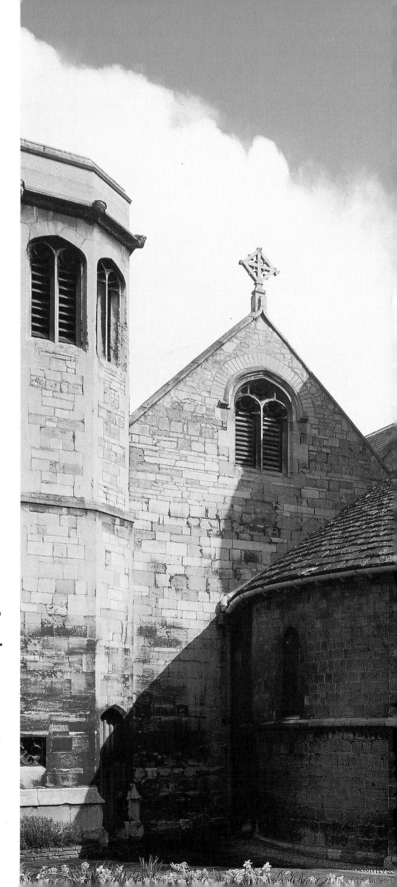

The Round Church The Church of the Holy Sepulchre acts as a visual punctuation mark when we turn the corner from Bridge Street into St John's Street. Most Cambridge people would not recognise the church under the above name. The them it is always known as, 'The Round Church'. Its roundness sets it apart from all other churches in the town and places it in a select group of circular medieval English churches. The land was granted around 1130 by Abbot Reinald of Ramsey to the 'fraternity of the Holy Sepulchre' who, like the Templars chose a round plan for its supposed associations with the Holy Sepulchre and the Holy Land. Its present external appearance with a conical roof we owe to the architect Anthony Salvin and the Cambridge Camden Society, a band of enthusiastic 19th century restorers. Little stood in the way of whatever they imagined to have been the original state of a building, and whether this jaunty peaked cap that they imposed upon the church bears any relation to what could have been seen here in the Middle Ages is questionable.

Behind the Round Church we glimpse the red brick Union built in 1866 the first of Alfred Waterhouse's works in Cambridge. The heart of the building and the Union's Society raison d'etre is the debating chamber where fledgling parliamentarians can cut their teeth on fellow undergraduates and on politicians returning from the cruel world outside to the quiet haunts of their youth only to be savaged by these young tyros.

Cette église circulaire, construite au XII. siècle, est l'une des très rares du même genre en Angleterre.

Diese Rundkirche aus dem 12. Jahrhundert ist eine von den sehr wenigen dieser Art in England.

この12世紀に建てられた円型の教会は、英国でもこのようなタイプのものとしては非常にめずらしいものの一つです

Jesus College Chapel In 1496 John Alcock, Bishop of Ely, obtained leave from Henry VII to suppress the Priory of St Radegund. He cited in justification of this move the dilapidation of its buildings, the alienation of its property and the diminution of its revenues, as well as the dissolute disposition and incontinency of the nuns. Doubt has been cast on the genuine nature of the reasons adduced, and it seems quite likely that Alcock presented the facts less than justly in order to bring about the foundation of his new college, Jesus College. The cloister of the nunnery was converted for the college's use. Thus Jesus is the only Cambridge college to possess a cloister running round all four sides of a court. The college chapel is the eastern half of the nunnery church. The western bays became the Master's Lodge.

In the religious vicissitudes of the 16th and 17th century ornaments were removed from and replaced in the chapel with the ebb and flow of the religious tide. In 1645 William Dowsing swept away everything in an iconoclastic fury, the organ alone being successfully hidden in the Master's orchard. The gaily painted organ case that we see here was part of the restoration of the chapel undertaken by A. W. Pugin in 1846-9. He also inserted the three lancet windows which look so convincingly Early English.

Jesus College et sa chapelle faisaient autrefois partie d'un couvent du moyen âge.

Das Jesus College und seine Kapelle bildeten einst einen Teil eines mittelalterlichen Nonnenklosters.

ジーゼス・カレッジとその教会は、一時は中世紀の尼僧院の一部でもありました

Pèpys Library, Magdalen College The great diarist and reformer of the Royal Navy, Samuel Pepys, had been at Magdalen as a student. In 1724 his old college received on the death of Pepys' nephew, Mr Jackson, the books which had been left by Pepys in 1708, one of the finest bequests that any college has ever received. Perhaps it was the bellyful of their beer — 'The best I ever drank' — enjoyed on a visit in 1668 as much as memories of his student days which persuaded him to his generosity.

The building which houses the collection had been begun much earlier. Part may date from the 16th century possibly as a first step towards a second court which was never achieved. At any rate in 1679 Robert Hooke made a 'draught' for the building and in 1679 a fellow of Magdalen writes to Pepys about building progress. Inside the 3,000 volumes of Pepys' collection are kept in the bookcases designed for Pepys himself in 1666. In this solidly, commodious setting we can benefit from the 'infinite pains, and time, and cost employed in my collecting'. The manuscript of his diary was included in the bequest and the entry for 24 August 1666 will tell us 'of the most extraordinary satisfaction' he felt upon the arrival at his London house of the 'new presses' for his books. He kept Simpson, who delivered them, with him until it was dark, hanging drawings and rearranging books in 'as noble a closett as any man hath and light enough — though indeed it would be better to have had a little more light'.

Samuel Pepys, le célèbre auteur d'un journal intime, fit don de sa bibliothèque au Magdalene College en 1708.

Der berühmte englische Chronist Samuel Pepys schenkte 1708 seine Bibliothek dem Magdalene College.

英国の有名な日記作家、サミュエル・ピープスは1708年にマグダレン・カレッジに彼の蔵書を寄贈しました

King's from the Backs in the snow On a crisp, winter's day we look across the Backs at the lawns of King's College. King's Chapel's stern splendour is set against the classical weight of the Fellow's Building designed by James Gibbs in 1723.

In 1447 the Mayor and Corporation had granted the land west of the river to the college. This area known as Butts Close was always intended for recreation and not for building. The path on the right winds in a sinuously picturesque manner to the bridge connecting the Backs to the college. To its left in the foreground of our picture lies Scholar's Piece where animals still graze in summer. It is a charmingly arranged landscape vista which is closely akin to the great parks surrounding 18th century country houses but it is not the enclosed and cloistered world which Henry VI imagined.

These are petty quibbles when one contemplates the size of what was achieved. Wordsworth well answered the critics of such magnificence.

> *Tax not the royal saint with vain expense,*
> *With ill-matched aims the Architect who planned,*
> *Albeit labouring for a scanty band*
> *Of white-robed Scholars only — this immense*
> *And glorious work of fine intelligence!*

The expense has been enormous, but in this century King's has been supremely fortunate in the possession of John Maynard Keynes as bursar of the college. Arguments may rage about his economic theories but there can be no doubting the investing skills with which he rebuilt the finances of King's.

King's College vu de "Cambridge Backs" un froid jour d'hiver.

Das King's College, an einem frischen Wintertag von der rückseitig der Colleges liegenden Allee gesehen.

寒さのきびしい冬の日にケンブリッジ・バックスから眺めるキングス・カレッジ

BIBLIOGRAPHY

Cambridge: A Brief History, J. W. Clark; 1890

Cambridge and its Story, Arthur Gray; 1912

Cambridge and its Colleges, A. Hamilton Thompson;
Little Guides, 1898

Architectural History of the University of Cambridge,
Willis and Clark; 4 volumes : 1886/7

City of Cambridge, Royal Commission on Historical
Monuments; 2 volumes : 1959

City and University of Cambridge, volume 3,
Victoria County History; 1959

Buildings of England: Cambridgeshire,
Nikolaus Pevsner; 1970

Period Piece — A Cambridge Childhood,
Gwen Raverat; 1952

CENTRAL PART OF THE MAP BY WILLIAM CUSTANCE, 1798

AA	Peterhouse	P	Emmanuel College
B	Clare College	Q	Sidney Sussex College
C	Pembroke College	R	Public Schools and Library
D	Corpus Christi College	S	Senate House
E	Trinity Hall	T	Botanic Gardens
F	Gonville and Caius College	a	King's College Chapel
GG	King's College	b	Great St Mary's Church
H	Queens' College	c	St Michael's Church
I	St Catharine's College	d	All Saints' Church
K	Jesus College	e	Holy Sepulchre Church
L	Christ's College	f	St Clement's Church
M	St John's College	i	Holy Trinity Church
N	Magdalene College	k	St Andrew's Church
O	Trinity College	l	St Edward's Church

m	St. Bene't's Church
n	St Botolph's Church
o	Little St Mary's Church
q	Shire Hall
r	Town Hall
s	Post Office
t	Free School
uu	Almshouses
w	Anabaptists' Meeting House
y	Site of the Old Bridge
z	Independents' Meeting House
B	Hobson's Conduit
C	Radegund Manor House